MW00929184

ワードえんへ

合氣道祥平塾

菅沼守人

Praise for the book that has been
helping people deal with the
modern world for years.

There is a moment in your life when you stop for a while.
When that happens, pick any page on this book and read it.
It sure will give you "courage" and "spiritual nourishment".

Masahiro Hashimoto
Dentist
Aikido 7th Dan
Japan

I have studied under Sugenuma Sensei for 41 years. He has taught me
how to "live in the moment" through Aikido.
It is 'here and now" in the eternal lapse of time in the infinite universe.
Now, the book, "Be Lively, Right Now, Right Here", has been translated
into English. I recommend many people worldwide to read the book
and use the guidance from it to lead a long fruitful life.

*Isamu Takeshita
Municipal Government Officer
Aikido 7th Dan
Japan*

"Be Lively, Right Here, Right Now" is a collection of wise phrases that Sugenuma Sensei has often quoted in his Aikido, Japanese calligraphy, and Zen meditation classes. Each phrase is hand-written with Sensei's elegant and powerful calligraphy with a simple commentary. The book has been an indispensable guide for improving and maintaining my way of life, not only as an Aikido instructor, but also as a member of the uncertain modern society. All the phrases written by Sensei resonate in the heart and nourish the spirit. Recommended as a guide to a better life for anyone.

Masaru Kiyota
Ph.D, University of British Columbia
Chief Instructor, Vancouver Shomonkai Aikido Association
Aikido 4th Dan
Canada

This wonderful book by master Suganuma conveys the wisdom of many great teachers in a short and friendly way. Highly recommended.

Eli Lerman
Chief Instructor, Aikido Centre of Israel
Aikido 5th Dan
Israel

This book will bless your life.
It gives a good insight into Japanese morality; however, why makes it a really great book is the author's style of writing.

Tomoko Iohara
Japanese Translator for "Aikido Preparatory Exercises – Healthy Body, Healthy Mind"
Aikido 1st Dan
UK

Copyright © 2014 by Morito Suganuma

All rights reserved. This book or any portion thereof may not be
reproduced or used in any manner whatsoever without the express
written permission of the publisher except for the use of brief
quotations in a book review.

Published by Tamami Nakashimada

Please contact the publisher at sjacanada@gmail.com for more
information regarding copywrite and interviews.

First Printed in Japanese: January 2005
First Printed in English: August 2014

To book Morito Suganuma for demonstration and speaking
engagments, see contact details below or contact the publisher:

Aikido Shoheijuku
5-2-32 Naka, Hakata-ku
Fukuoka 812-0893 Japan
E-mail: shoheijuku@nifty.com

Translation: Yasuko Garlick, Yuko Ozawa
Layout and Design: DB Communications

ISBN-13: 978-1500734534

Printed in the United States of America
13   12   11   10   9 8 7 6 5 4 3 2 1

www.shoheijukubook.com

Be Lively,
Right Here,
Right Now

CONTENTS

Introduction _____ 12

Following a masters path _____ 14

"Men of today know everything,
yet they are too ignorant about themselves." _____ 19

"Every man is the architect of his own fortune." _____ 21

Even without sound and scent
The universe continues on
And repeats the lessons of the Buddhist scriptures _____ 23

"The true beauty of women lies within her character." ____ 25

It is always better to say "Thank you" and "I am sorry" as soon as possible. ___ 27

The keys to longevity is to go to bed early, rise early, be tidy
Eat less and refrain from sexual activities _____ 29

"To live a long life, eat simple meals, be honest, bathe daily, recite sutras,
And pass wind once in a while." _____ 31

If my mind can be seen in a mirror
It must be an ugly sight _____ 33

Seen on close approach, Mt Fuji is not so spectacular.
Perhaps Buddha and Confucius were the same. _____ 35

The world is filled with plenty of people
But it lacks virtuous ones _____ 37

Regardless of whether something is sharp or blunt
It is not to be disregarded
As we could use it properly as a drill or hammer _____ 39

Trouble comes out from the mouth, illness enters through it. ___ 41

Pleasure is when an unwelcome guest visits
Yet goes home after staying for just a short while _____ 43

CONTENTS

Not enough time? You must be joking. You are just unmotivated. _____ 45

Instead of traveling ten miles in one day
it is more enjoyable to travel ten miles in ten days _____ 47

Time lost cannot be recalled
And there will not be another dawning of the day _____ 49

If you look down, that would look more beautiful than making an excuse _____ 51

The movement of Universe is steady.
Likewise, a man of virtue exerts himself with perseverance. _____ 53

Treat others gently like the spring wind
Restrain yourself like the autumn frost _____ 55

Pray to God and Buddha for something selfish _____ 57

Sorrow and joy come from the same origin.
Both of them come from our own heart. _____ 59

Teaching face-to-face and learning face-to-face _____ 61

Actual Practice _____ 63

Parents always pray for their children,
but children do not pray for their parents. _____ 65

"A man and a cigarette, we can only tell whether they are good or not,
after they have turned into smoke." _____ 67

The more we polish it, the more it will shine
A man's character or a gemstone _____ 69

"He who knows does not speak.
He who speaks does not know." _____ 71

"Show them, tell them and let them do it.
Then praise them.
Otherwise, people will not do anything." _____ 73

CONTENTS

Don't scold children as you took the same path.
Don't laugh at the elderly as you will take the same path. _____ 75

If you think there is tomorrow
The most beautiful cherry blossom may be gone
In the storm in the middle of the night _____ 77

I will not lose to my wife, says a fool. _____ 79

Though there must be winds that it does not like,
The willow is still there. _____ 81

"It is relatively easy to die gracefully,
yet, it is extremely hard to age gracefully." _____ 83

I sit in Kotatsu* alone regretting how I talked too much _____ 85

An orchid becomes whiter
As it endures rain and wind _____ 87

Lazy people get busy when the evening approaches. _____ 89

"Diligence in the midst of activity is
immeasurably superior to diligence within tranquility." _____ 91

Whether this fall brings rain or storm
My job today is to weed the rice field _____ 93

"Yesterday's poem is today's farewell verse.
Today's poem is tomorrow's farewell verse." _____ 95

Always thought to live to hundred, free of ailments
Ninety six is far too early _____ 97

Getting angry once makes you one year older
Laughing once makes you one year younger _____ 99

"He who has a peaceful mind will live a long life." _____ 101

CONTENTS

With the first cup, a man drinks liquor
With the second cup, liquor drinks liquor
With the third cup, liquor swallows up the man _____ 103

No matter how many drinks he had,
Confucius never loses control of himself _____ 105

If you are to drink, drink with a true man
Your time will be better spent than reading books for ten years _____ 107

So long as your heart follows the true way
God shall protect you even if you do not offer a prayer. _____ 109

"Do your best and leave the rest to the Mandate of Heaven." _____ 111

One tries to dig a well
But gives up just a foot before hitting water
What a pity _____ 113

People grow old
Controlled by money meant to be used _____ 115

Everybody always say they are busy.
Yet, they have a vacant look in their eyes. _____ 117

Sleep in the morning, have a nap before going to bed early,
wake up once in a while, dozing off. _____ 119

Those who study in their youth will achieve something during
their middle age years
Those who study in their middle age will not decline in their old age
Those who study in their old age will not be forgotten after their passing ____ 121

Do not ask me about the secret for success
Try your best to accomplish each and every thing you must do _____ 123

"The path of duty is near, and men seek it afar.
The work of duty is easy, and men seek it in something difficult." _____ 125

CONTENTS

Do the ordinary things in the ordinary way. _____ 127

"Loss is enlightenment.
Gain is delusion." _____ 129

"Tips for good mental and physical health for busy people.
Happiness, appreciation, and a secret act of charity." _____ 131

"Every man over forty is responsible for his face." _____ 133

"A man should have free and easy manners." _____ 135

"One's destiny lies within his personality,
– a phrase like this is not a random remark." _____ 137

"Jump over a ditch without hesitation.
If you think it is dangerous, you will fall into it." _____ 139

For the time being
Just think about today
As the past is gone, and the future is unknown _____ 141

A mind to nurture people for the society
is also a mind to nurture oneself. _____ 143

"Do not take advantage of someone's weakness." _____ 145

If you can one day recreate yourself,
Do so from day to day.
Let there be daily recreation. _____ 147

The second generation copy their parents. _____ 149

"Up until now, I thought death was for other people.
But now that I am dying, I can't stand it." _____ 151

"The God of Wealth" knows what is enough
Ebisu never fishes for two snappers _____ 153

CONTENTS

Average is just average.
Unless you stand out,
You are never extraordinary. _____ 155

Do everything in earnest. _____ 157

Look at the shadow in both of my eyes, my friend
Silence conceal the sorrow _____ 159

Though the rows of Buddhas have the merciful looks
They are also bearing all the pains _____ 161

Never blame Heaven or people
Look back at your own faults _____ 163

The more rice an ear has
The lower it hangs _____ 165

Zanshin is beautiful. _____ 167

Do not do bad things.
Do good things. _____ 169

"Thanks to my parents, teachers, and friend,
I am who I am today.
Never think you did everything by yourself." _____ 171

One chance in a lifetime _____ 173

Profile of Morito Suganuma _____ 175

INTRODUCTION

Live Life, Right Here, Right Now

This is the motto of our dojo, Shoheijuku.
As it is said, "a day is a miniature copy of life", our lives are the accumulation of each day. Each day is also the accumulation of each moment. To live each day of our lives to the fullest means to live each moment to the fullest. This also means that we live our entire lives to the fullest.

Many people say they are busy
Yet, they have a vacant look in their eyes

I feel that many people are pressed for time and have become consumed by a daily grind, which takes away their awareness of active life, and they are about to lose their breathing space.

I travel a lot throughout the year to visit people. This book is a collection of a little over 70 quotes and my thoughts, including some of the questions I was asked while visiting various dojos and talking with younger people over drinks. It was originally written for our dojo members under different title, and many of the quotes and thoughts are lessons for myself as well.

**"It's OK to go to sleep when you are sleepy,
buy do your best when you are awake."**

It was a guiding principle of Takaba Juku where Mitsuru Toyama Sensei studied during his formative years.

**It is such a waste of time if we spend our days
not knowing if we are awake or asleep.**

I hope everybody I have come across over the years live each day fully and lively.

Morito Suganuma

FOLLOWING A MASTER'S PATH

Sensei stands with Master Morihei Ueshiba, the first Doshu, at Ueno Station in Tokyo on their way to Dojo in Iwama, Ibaraki Prefecture.

Morihei Ueshiba was the founder of the Japanese martial art of aikido. He is often referred to as "the founder" Kaiso or Osensei, "Great Teacher". In 1919, Ueshiba joined the Omoto-kyo movement in Ayabe, serving as a martial arts instructor and opening his first dojo. The following year, he experienced a great spiritual enlightenment, stating that, "a golden spirit sprang up from the ground, veiled my body, and changed my body into a golden one." After this experience, his martial arts skill and focus appeared to greatly increase.

Sensei meets with his Zen master, Shinryu Umeda, for a Bonenkai party in Fukuoka Prefecture on December 17, 1995.

A Bonenkai is a traditional year-end party where you celebrate the year and divest yourself of any hard feelings from that year.

Fukuoka is part of Japan's south-western island area, and is approximately 1000km form Tokyo.

FOLLOWING A MASTER'S PATH

Sensei with Master Kisshomaru Ueshiba, the second Doshu on July 26, 1994.

Master Kisshomaru was the son of Morihei Ueshiba, founder of Aikido, and became the international leader of Aikido after his father's death. As his father was the first Doshu, he became the second Doshu, and after his death, his son Moriteru Ueshiba became the third Doshu.

Iemoto is a Japanese term used to refer to the founder or current Head Master of a certain school of traditional Japanese art. The word iemoto is also used to describe a system of familial generations in traditional Japanese arts. The Iemoto system is characterized by a hierarchical structure and the supreme authority of the Iemoto, who has inherited the secret traditions of the school from the previous Iemoto.

Sensei with Mr. Kisaburo Osawa, his Aikido master, at Dazaifu Denmangu Shrine in Dazaifu City, Fukuoka for sight-seeing after the second public demonstrations of Shoheijuku in April, 1988.

現代人はどんなことでも
　　よく知っている
ただ・自分のことを
あまりにも知らなすぎる

トインビー

"Men of today know everything, yet they are too ignorant about themselves."

Arnold Toynbee

We sometimes say, "Look how he dresses despite his age!" or "How foolish of him at his age to do such a thing."

It is easy for us to look at others and criticize them, while it is difficult to do the same when it comes to our own.

As the saying goes, "By other's faults, wise men correct their own."

At the entrance to a Zen temple, we often see a sign that says "Kyakkashoko" or "Kankyakka."

These words literally mean to place your shoes neatly when you take you shoes off. But it also implies to look upon ourselves before criticizing others.

This reminds me of what Morihei Ueshiba Sensei, the founder of Aikido, used to say.

"Aikido is a martial art of self improvement."

各人は
己の運命の作者である

サルスティウス

"Every man is the architect
of his own fortune."

Sallustius

Successful people succeed because they do things that lead them to success, whereas unsuccessful people fail because they do things that lead them to failure.

This also applies to our own destiny. If we always look on the negative side of things, we will become pessimistic ourselves.

Negative people are bound to have doomed destiny.

"Our destiny lies in our personality."

音もなく
香もなく常に天地は
書かざる経を
くりかえしつつ

二宮尊徳

"Even without sound and scent
The universe continues on
And repeats the lessons of the Buddhist scriptures."

Sontoku Ninomiya

Eiji Yoshikawa once said, "everybody but myself is my teacher".

All things in the universe teach us something. There is nothing in the universe that is not a written or spoken word telling us something.

Rather than reading and listening to the letters and words superficially, we should sense and absorb everything from our surrounding by feeling the flow and the atmosphere of Mother Nature.

The Book of Changes states: "A man of virtue keeps working hard, as the revolution of the universe goes steadily. " We should keep working hard every day without going against the movement of Great Nature.

女性の美は性格の中にある

ロダン

"The true beauty of women lies within her character."

Rodin

The infamous three words that we often hear from incompetent women (men as well) are;

Because,
But,
Anyhow

Let's avoid using these words.

The woman looking down bashfully is more beautiful than those who give excuses.

「ありがとう」と「すみません」は
早い方がいい

It is always better to say "Thank you" and "I am sorry" as soon as possible.

When we receive a letter or gift, we should show our appreciation without delay. It could be by mail or telephone call.

We should be careful not to plan to send a thank-you note when we have more time, and then unintentionally forget to do so.

Be assertive when you believe you are right. However, you should apologize from the bottom of your heart without hesitation when you realize you made a mistake.

There are people who do not apologize easily. The Analects of Confucius says when a small-timer makes mistakes he finds excuses to cover himself up.

長生きは
宵寝早起き きれいずき
食を控えて
色を控えよ

白隠

The keys to longevity is
to go to bed early, rise early, be tidy,
eat less and refrain from sexual activities

Hakuin

There are two extraordinary things in Suruga:
Mount Fuji and Hakuin from Hara

As praised in this poem, Hakuin Zenji was said to be the distinguished Zen priest, who could appear once in every five hundred years. However, he suffered a life-threatening "Zen sickness" when he was young, and it was feared that he would never recover from the illness.

One day, determined to overcome the illness, he used techniques called "Soft-butter Healing Method" and "Introspective Meditation Method." Having restored the health of his body and mind, he devoted the rest of his life to benefiting others and lived until the ripe age of 84.

This must have been his secret of longevity though his own life experience.

長命は
粗食正直日湯陀羅尼
おりおり下風
あそばさるべし

天海

30

"To live a long life, eat simple meals, be honest, bathe daily, recite sutras, and pass wind once in a while"

Tenkai

Tenkai Sojo, a trusted advisor to Ieyasu Tokugawa, was called the Prime Minister in Black and lived to the great age of 108.

When asked of the secrets to perpetual youth and longevity, he told them, "Eat simple meals, be honest, bathe daily, recite sutras, and pass wind occasionally."

Bitto means to take a bath daily to clean oneself and improve blood circulation. Darani is to recite sutras.
Kafu is the passing of wind. He may have been suggesting one should take it easy and be relaxed enough to pass wind in front of his followers instead of thinking so hard about politics with a frown.

This reminds me of another poem;
The wind of a daughter-in-law
Goes round and round in the entire body

One should not suppress it too much
(there is a time and place for everything, though).

我が心
鏡に映るものならば
さぞや姿の
みにくかるらん

What if our mind can be displayed in the mirror?
It gives me a shiver at the very thought of it.

My Zen teacher, Shinryu Umeda Zenji used to say,

"The more you dig into your own heart,
the more you should see how immature you are."

来てみれば
さほどでもなし富士の山
釈迦や孔子も
かくやありなん

村田清風

34

**Seen on close approach, Mt Fuji is not so spectacular.
Perhaps Buddha and Confucius were the same.**

Murata Seifu

This is a poem by Seifu Murata who trained Shoin Yoshida.

He is certainly not implying that the Buddha and Confucius were not great men. Most likely he is suggesting to us the idea of "he is human and I am also human."

A crossroad in our life is when we consider "I can become that" or "I cannot possibly become that."

天下に最も多きは人なり

最も少なきも人なり

黒田如水

36

The world is filled with plenty of people but it lacks virtuous ones

Josui Kuroda

A wise monarch, Yozan Uesugi, composed a similar poem
There are many human beings, but no one excelled among them.
You should become the one. You should raise one.

When Shojiro Goto lamented about the lack of respectable people, the revered old Mitsuru Toyama encouraged him by saying, "If there are no good people out there, you just have to become one."

鋭きも
鈍きも共に捨てがたし
錐と鎚とに使い分けなば

廣瀬淡窓

38

Regardless of whether something is sharp or blunt, it is not to be disregarded
As we could use it properly as a drill or hammer

Tanso Hirose

Josui Kuroda admonished his son, Nagamasa, saying, "Do not talk about right and wrong of others. That depends on those who handle them." I believe that those who can bring out the best in others are the ones who can bring out the best in themselves.

Don't give up on people just because of their faults.
Look at a bitter persimmon. It turns into a sweet persimmon.

禍（わざわい）は口より出て
病は口より入る

Trouble comes out from the mouth, illness enters through it.

"Break wind and control your bottom." Once it is out, it is done and irreversible.
I myself often regret talking too much without meaning to do so.

I sit in Kotatsu* alone
Regretting how I talked too much

*Kotatsu
A knee-high table with an electric warmer installed under the removable top board, which is used with a cover during the winter in Japan.

楽しみは
いやなる人の来たりしが
長くもおらで
帰りけるとき

橘曙覧

Pleasure is when an unwelcome guest visits
Yet goes home after staying for just a short while

Tachibana no Akemi

In this world, it is a pleasure to have people come and visit me
As long as it is not you Rai Sanyo's poem goes like this.
One should leave before someone hints at it.

"The longer you live,
the more chance you
embarrass yourself.
It would be ideal for a man
to die just a little shy of the age of forty."

Harvest of Leisure

時間がない？

冗談でしょうやる気がない

Not enough time? You must be joking. You are just unmotivated.

In the following poem, Dogen Zenji writes
Although we often spend our time doing nothing particular
We tend to spend little time seeking for the truth

Issai Sato also writes in his book, Genshiroku, that most people spend
from 70 to 80% of their day doing unnecessary things. If they waste their
time doing useless things, it is no wonder they have less time to do really
important things.

"The world became a much smaller place thanks to
the advances in transportation. However, when you
wonder the reason for driving in a big hurry,
it is to play Pachinko (Japanese pinball).
They are speeding up to waste more time."

Kodo Sawaki

一日に十里の道をゆくよりも

十日に十里

ゆくぞたのしき

Instead of traveling ten miles in one day
It is more enjoyable to travel ten miles in ten day

Master Taido Matsubara of Rinzai Sect, born in 1907, said to have valued and practiced three rules that he lived by.
They are, not to overexert yourself, not to waste anything, and not to be lazy.

He who goes calmly, goes healthily; he who goes healthily, goes far.

Saburo Shiroyama

The key here is making a little daily effort.

盛年重ねて来たらず

一日再び晨（あした）なり難し

陶淵明

Time lost cannot be recalled
And there will not be another dawning of the day

Tao Yuan Ming

In his book, "Genshiroku," Issai Sato writes as follows.

When people are young and full of energy, they do not know how precious time is. Even if they know it, they just do not to place great value on time.

Only after they pass the age of forty, they realize for the first time how precious time is. However, their physical strength gradually starts to decline around this time.

Therefore, they must be determined to learn or train when they are still young, and work really hard. Otherwise, it is no use regretting something they have not done later on.

うつむけば
言い訳よりも美しき

If you look down, that would look more beautiful than making an excuse

Just as children never bother to dry their wet clothes
You ended your life defencelessly.

This is a poem composed by Kaishu Katsu, mourning over the death of Takamori Saigo. To what extent can we stay silent against slanders?

People tend to justify themselves to protect their names.

"A small persons making a mistake will always embellish it."

The Analects of Confucius

(When a man of small character makes a mistake, he is sure to try to cover it up and embellish it.)

Little things please little minds.

天行は健なり
君子は以て
自ら彊めて息まず

易経

52

**The movement of Universe is steady.
Likewise, a man of virtue
exerts himself with perseverance.**

I Ching (The Book of Changes)

There is no confusion in the flow of dharma or the revolution of Universe. Likewise, it is the way of a wise man to work hard with perseverance. "Learn from laws of nature" is a teaching of Morihei Ueshiba Sensei, the founder of Aikido.

春風以て人に接し
秋霜以て自ら粛む

佐藤一斉

54

Treat others gently like the spring wind
Restrain yourself like the autumn frost

Issai Sato

Try to be kind to others like the spring wind, but be strict to yourself like the autumn frost.

However, I tend to get it the wrong way round, as "treating ourselves gently like the spring wind and being strict to others like the autumn frost."

When spring wind blows
Toukichirou is here

神佛に手前勝手を申しあげ

Pray to God and Buddha for something selfish

The poem by Sugawara no Michizane, the god of education, says
As far as your heart follows the true way, the god will protect you even if you
do not pray.

Have I been doing the right thing so that god will protect me?
Have I been doing things that god would disapprove of?

A traditional folk song from Kagoshima, "Kushikino Sanosa" goes
People pray to the sunrise, but no one prays to the sunset.

苦も楽も
生まれし先は一つところ
いずれも己が心より出ず

Sorrow and joy come from the same origin.
Both come from our own heart.

As the Jewish proverb goes
"If you break a leg, be thankful that you did not break both legs. If you break both legs, be thankful that you did not break your neck."

In order to have a better life, success or happiness, stop having negative and unproductive thoughts.
Most of the times, things turn out to be better than you think, when you think positive and be optimistic.

"Don't count what you have lost. Maximize what you have left." said Dr. Guttmann, the founder of the Paralympics.

面授面受

Teaching face-to-face and learning face-to-face

Giving face-to-face and receiving face-to-face. It is a foundation of educating people.

Umeda Zenji told me that whether you have hundreds or thousands of students, always attend to each student, as if you are teaching him one-on-one.
I try my best to practice that at the best of my ability.

It is hard to provide a truly compassionate education with the modern production-line education where students are taught systematically in the lump.
Regardless of how many children or students there are, we should always strive for one-on-one teaching and learning.

実践躬行

Actual Practice

We say we have to protect Earth from the destruction of nature, while we continue polluting air and water. Trees are being cut down one after another, and mountains are levelled.

We emphasize the importance of peace and happiness, yet conflicts, murders and wars never end. Things that need to be solved are probably sitting right in front of us. They may be simple things to do, but it is important for each and every one of us to actually do it.

When the late Emperor Hirohito was still the Crown Prince, Jugo Sugiura, Professor of Ethics, always told him after each lecture. "Generally, no success is achieved by merely talking about ethics. The valuable part of ethics is only one thing; "Actual Practice." A journey of a thousand miles begins with one single step.

父母は常に子を念ずれど

子は父母を念ぜず

Parents always pray for their children, but children do not pray for their parents.

The following sentences are a part of the letter sent to Hideyo Noguchi from his mother, Shika, when he earned his doctorate degree in medicine.

I pray facing west. I pray facing east. I pray facing north. I pray facing south. I cut out salt from my diet on the first day of the month. I ask Eisho, a Buddhist priest, to pray on the first day of the month. I will never forget praying even if I forget everything else...

It is unconditional love, without demanding anything in return. This must be the love of parents.

人とタバコのよしあしは
煙になりてのちにこそ知れ

山本玄峰

"A man and a cigarette, we can only tell whether they are good or not, after they have turned into smoke."

Genpo Yamamoto

Genpo Yamamoto, a Zen master, often said to his disciples.

"You can tell a man's worth at 80 rather than 70, at 90 rather than 80, at 100 rather than 90, and what he leaves behind after his death rather than 100."

Tesshu Yamaoka also laughed and said, "It will be five hundred years from now when my name will become known."

I feel that they are slightly (actually greatly) different class from those who always try to do this and that, hoping to be praised or receiving a medal of honour in their lifetimes.

磨いたら
磨いただけの光あり
性根玉でも何の玉でも

山本玄峰

The more we polish it, the more it will shine
A man's character or a gemstone

Genpo Yamamoto

This is also a poem by Genpo Yamamoto.

A gem will surely shine when polished because of its own nature. Humans are the same if we know how to bring out our true inner strength. Then, our brilliance will eventually shine through.

Nowadays, a quick result may be more common than an the idea of carefully and thoroughly working something out. However, something which gives immediate results often fails quickly.

It is impossible to make something shine without polishing. "An uncut gem does not sparkle," as the saying goes.

知る者は言わず
言う者は知らず

老子

"He who knows does not speak.
He who speaks does not know."

Lao Tzu

In the Analects of Confucius, Master Zeng says

"Each day I examine my conscience many times.
Have I failed to be faithful in planning for others?
Have I failed to be trustworthy in company with friends?
Have I taught something I have not mastered to others (pretending to know it all)?"
It almost makes me blush with shame just thinking about it.

When I speak
My lips are chilled
With an autumn wind

やってみせて
言ってきかせてさせてみて
ほめてやらねば
人は動かじ

山本五十六

"Show them, tell them and let them do it.
Then praise them.
Otherwise, people will not do anything."

Isoroku Yamamoto

There is a senryu (satirical poem) that goes like this
Despite being shown how to do it
Never does anything, even with praise
The new generation

We also say that even a pig will climb a tree if you praise for it.

It is embarrassing to see one overly flattering another. However, it is also sad if we cannot feel anything or cannot praise anybody, when we see someone's merit and good point.

Finding strength and good quality in others, rather than finding faults and weakness leads to enriching our own mind.

If the leader sets himself right, everybody will follow him without his command.
If he does not set himself right, nobody will follow his command.

The Analects of Confucius

Nobody will follow a man who orders others to do things that he cannot himself.

子供叱るな
来た路じゃもの
年寄り笑うな
行く路じゃもの

Don't scold children, as you took the same path.
Don't laugh at the elderly,
as you will take the same path.

When children whine and complain, their parents scold them and say, "You are being unreasonable."

Actually, most of the parents themselves are being unreasonable, too. This is called ignorance.

Kodo Sawaki

明日ありと
思う心のあだざくら
夜半に嵐の
吹かぬものかは

親鸞

**If you think there is tomorrow
The most beautiful cherry blossom may be gone
In the storm in the middle of the night**

Shinran

Lazy people will say, "maybe not today but tomorrow."
This hits a sore spot.
A day is a miniature copy of life, as they say. Perhaps what we have to do
today should be finished today.

女房に
負けるものかと
馬鹿が言い

I will not lose to my wife, says a fool.

The words you should never say once you are married are:
"I wish I didn't marry you."

"I would like to be with you again if I were to be born again in the next life."
Do you think your wife will tell you that?

氣に入らぬ風もあろうに柳かな

仙厓

80

Though there must be winds that it does not like, The willow is still there.

Sengai

It is said that a willow does not break under the weight of snow. "Flexible body and gentle heart" is one of the goals in practicing Makko-Ho (a system of stretching exercises). Being flexible does not mean being weak or spineless. Instead, it refers to being flexible with straight backbone.

美しく死ぬことは
さほど難しいことではない
しかし、美しく老いることは
至難の業だ

アンドレ・ジード

"It is relatively easy to die gracefully, yet, it is extremely hard to age gracefully."

André Gide

It is definitely an unhappy life if it was miserable in one's later years, although it was spectacular in his youth. Conversely, we can say that one had a happy life if he leads a fruitful life in his later years, although he had a series of hardships in the past.

The Roots of Wisdom (Saikontan) says,
"To evaluate a man, just look at his last years."
The important thing is how we live in our later years.

饒舌を
悔いるひとりの炉燵かな

I sit in Kotatsu* alone regretting how I talked too much.

Ryokan (a Zen priest and a poet in the Edo period) was not really fond of preaching others or talking about morals. However, he was very strict when it came to the usage of language. When asked by others, he would write "Lessons of Language Use" for them. A few of them are as follows.

1) Talking too much, 2) Talking too long, 3) Talking too fast, 4) Talking in a hurry, 5) Bragging about one's own deeds, 6) Cutting others off when they are still talking, 7) Making a promise easily, 8) Telling others what you will give them before actually giving it to them, 9) Telling others what you gave to someone, 10) Wanting to give a lecture often, 11) Talking bluntly about things that someone wants to hide, 12) Whispering into someone's ear, 13) Wanting to use foreign words, 14) Talking about spiritual enlightenment, 15) Smoothing over one's own faults, etc.

*Kotatsu – A knee-high table with an electric warmer installed under the removable top board, which is used with a cover during the winter in Japan

雨に風に
逢うほど蘭の白さかな

An orchid becomes whiter
As it endures rain and wind

Shikanosuke Yamanaka, looking at the moon, while praying and said,
"God, please allow me to have seven misfortunes and eight pains."

Banzan Kumazawa also made a poem:
Let all troubles come upon me and test my limit
A human being grows stronger through experiencing hardships in life
Flowers in a greenhouse are feeble

However, there are some people who rather become mean after going
through tough times. Even if they go through the same hardship, there will
be a world of difference between those who make good use of the experience
and those who do not. When we run into a pain or a hardship in our lives,
it would be wonderful if we can think of it as a trial given by God and face it
bravely.

夕方になると
怠け者は忙しくなる

Lazy people get busy when the evening approaches.

Sometimes, we tell ourselves that we do not need to rush and can go slowly, as we have plenty of time. Later, we often realize that it is already evening and we must hurry.

"Time waits for no one. To waste time is a great shame."

"Our 50s is like 3 o'clock in the afternoon. The sun is still up, but we must hurry.", quoted Goethe.

We all have to be careful not to panic towards the evening of our lives.

動中の工夫は
静中の工夫に勝ること
百千億倍

白隠

"Diligence in the midst of activity is immeasurably
superior to diligence within tranquility."

Hakuin

"There are some people who think that Zen means just sitting still. That is
like a fox sitting in a den that will not come out. That is no good. Go coax it
out with something it wants."(Hakuin).

Hakuin Zenji (Zen master) preached that practice in the midst of activity is
ten trillion times more important than just meditating. How can we make
full use of Zen in the midst of everyday life? It is certainly important to sit in
a quiet place, but we should not avoid the hustle and bustle all the time.

What is important is how we apply Zen in the daily bustling of life.

この秋は
雨か嵐か知らねども
今日のつとめに
田草取るなり

二宮尊徳

Whether this fall brings rain or storm
My job today is to weed the rice field

Sontoku Ninomiya

When I just started Zen meditation, Umeda Zenji told me that there was no yesterday or tomorrow. He also told me to put my best effort into right here and now, as what I had was exactly that. It may sound exaggerated if I say I saw the light. However, I remember it was as though the mist in front of my eyes had suddenly lifted.

It is important that what we ought to do today should be done today, instead of putting it off till tomorrow.

昨日の発句は今日の辞世

今日の発句は明日の辞世

芭蕉

94

"Yesterday's poem is today's farewell verse. Today's poem is tomorrow's farewell verse."

Basho

When Basho Matuso was asked what his farewell poem was, he said, "Yesterday's poem is today's farewell verse. Today's poem is tomorrow's farewell verse." He also added that, of all the poems he had read, there was nothing that could not be a farewell verse. It is like "A day is a miniature copy of one's life."

Today is the day to complete a piece of work called today.

Yoshio Toi

百までは
何でもないと思いしに
九十六とはあまり早死

英
一桂

Always thought to live to hundred, free of ailments
Ninety six is far too early

Ikkei Hanabusa

His disciple who were requesting for his last injunctions at his deathbed approached Sengai, a Buddhist priest, also known as Sengai-san. He smiled and said, "I don't want to die."

In disappointment, the disciple said, "What did you say? How can a distinguished priest from Hakata like you say such a thing?"
Sengai, while still smiling, said, "Seriously, I don't want to die."

Umeda Zenji once said, "I've heard Sengai Osho said that he did not want to die. I believe that is what he actually said. For myself, when my time comes, I want to say the same, but while wearing a smile on my face. This same 'I don't want to die' has a totally different meaning between a person reduced to plea and a person calmly saying this. There lies a world of difference.

一怒一老

一笑一若

Getting angry once makes you one year older
Laughing once makes you one year younger

This is a Chinese proverb that says when we get angry once, we will become a year older, and when we laugh once, we will become one year younger.

Dr. Kenzo Futaki, who became an uchideshi (apprentice) to Morihei Ueshiba Sensei when he was in his 60s, wrote in his self-admonition "Enmei Jukku (Ten phrases for prolonging life)".

1. Eat less meat and more vegetables
2. Use less salt and more vinegar
3. Use less sugar and eat more fruit
4. Eat less and chew more
5. Wear fewer clothes and take a bath often
6. Drive less and walk more
7. Worry less and sleep longer
8. Less anger but more laughter
9. Less word but more action
10. Suppress your desire but offer to do more

These lessons are not about "do not," but are about "do less." Dr. Futaki practiced them and lived to the ripe old age of 93. He also kept practicing Aikido even when he passed the age of 80.

心平らかなれば寿し

白楽天

"He who has a peaceful mind will live a long life."

Hakurakuten

Ekiken Kaibara, known for his book "Yojokun (Lessons on Nurturing Life)," says, "Be calm and let your spirit harmonize. This is the way to nurture your body and soul."

"Saikontan (The Root of Wisdom)," also says,"Lucks come to those who have gentle and peaceful mind." Perhaps those who has calm mind naturally attract happiness. It seems that many of the people who live a long life are reposeful. They do not seem to worry about or fuss over little things. The Heart Sutra also says that if one's mind is free of distractions, he will have no fear. Managing your own mind is a milestone to longevity.

一盃は人酒を飲み
二盃は酒酒を飲み
三盃は酒人を飲む

With the first cup, a man drinks liquor
With the second cup, liquor drinks liquor
With the third cup, liquor swallows up the man

We all know that we should enjoy our drinks but not get drunk against our better judgment. We sometimes end up with a hangover and are not able to work the next day. Losing control in drunkness can ruin the true value of drinking.

When we drink, we should make sure not only ourselves, but also others are having a good time. It would also be nice if it helps motivate us to work harder.

"It is best to rise from life as from a banquet, neither thirsty nor drunken."

Aristotle

酒は量なし
乱に及ばず

論語

No matter how many drinks he had, Confucius never loses control of himself

The Analects of Confucius

There is no specific limit to the amount of alcohol we can drink. However, we should not lose control of ourselves.

There are three moments when a man reveals his true self.
1) When he is drunk.
(Some people show behaviours that are out of their character.)

2) When he loses his temper.
(I thought he was always gentle and calm.)

3) When he gives out tips.
(He usually talks big.)

We have to be very cautious.

酒を飲むなら
大文夫と飲みゃれ
十年かけた読書に勝る

If you are to drink, drink with a true man
Your time will be better spent than
reading books for ten years

This is a poem Hanbei Takenaka sent to Kanbei Kurota. The Analects of Confucius says "No matter how much he drinks, Confucius never loses control of himself." Some will turn red after drinking a small amount of alcohol, while others will be fine even after drinking a large amount of alcohol. There is no fixed amount of alcohol we can drink, but we should not lose control of ourselves. It is up to each of us whether we treat it as the best of all medicines or a drink to turn you into a madman. Alcohol itself does not have a responsibility at all.

When drinking with a good friend, even a thousand gallons of alcohol is not enough.

When drinking with someone who talks worthless things, even half a word is a lot.

We can drink plenty of alcohol when we are drinking with a trusted friend. However, we do not want to say even a word or half a word when we drink with someone we do not get along.

心だに　誠の道に叶ひなば　祈らずとても　神や守らん

菅原道真

108

**So long as your heart follows the true way
God shall protect you even if you do not offer a prayer.**

Sugawara no Michizane

This is a poem by Sugawawa no Michizane who was known as the God of Wisdom.

No matter how much you pray to God to let you pass the test to get into that school, it will not come true if you do not have the ability.

In the real world, we only get in return of what we put into.
Have I been doing the right thing that God would be pleased?
Have I been doing things that God would disapprove?

人事を尽くして天命を待つ

胡寅

"Do your best and leave the rest to the Mandate of Heaven."

Koin

After you try your best, let God do the rest.

Are you saying you cannot do it, even though you have not actually tried?

Is there anything else you can do?

Look closely from the different perspectives and try again.

井戸を掘りて
あと一尺である水を
出ずとやめる
人ぞかなしき

One tries to dig a well
But gives up just a foot before hitting water
What a pity

Rikinosuke Ishikawa, an agricultural leader, also referred to as Sontoku Ninomiya of the Meiji era, said,

"If you dig a well, dig until it springs."
Do not give up half way through, but continue until you succeed.

"If you plan to travel 100 miles, consider you reach only half way when you travel past 90 miles."
We should not lose the focus when we are almost there.

使うべき
金に使われ老いにけり

People grow old
Controlled by money meant to be used

Confucius said,
"There is some pleasure in living in poverty like having plain food, drinking water, and using your arm as your pillow to sleep. However, it is transient and meaningless just like the cloud floating in the sky, if I become rich or promoted by doing something unjust."

There is no end to the news about someone ruining his own life because of a murder just to get some spending money for pleasure.

Money and things are something we use. We have to make sure we do not get controlled by them.

誰も彼も
口を開けば忙しと
言いつゝどこか
うつろなる眼よ

Everybody always say they are busy.
Yet, they have a vacant look in their eyes

In his book Genshiroku, Sato Issai says, "People nowadays have a habit
of saying they are busy. However, when we look at them, only a couple of
things out of 10 are important, and the rest are not. No wonder they are so
busy, as they consider those insignificant things important. Someone who
has high aspirations to achieve something should not fall into such a pitfall."

朝寝して
宵寝するまで昼寝して
時々起きて
居眠りをする

Sleep in the morning,
have a nap before going to bed early,
wake up once in a while, dozing off

Zeng Guo Fan from the end of Qing Dynasty told himself to get up immediately after waking up in the morning without staying in bed lazily, and not wishing for more time to sleep.

"Get up at dawn. Do not take time getting up."

Whether oversleeping or not greatly affects our work efficiency as well as our mentality. Rising early seems to strengthen our willpower.

I remember reading somewhere that the kanji character 朝 (asa - morning) consists of the four letters 十月十日 (totsukitouka - ten months and ten days).

There is a word 日新 (nisshin – new day). We would start anew every day, if we could welcome each morning feeling like we were just born.

少にして学べば
則ち壮にして為すことあり
壮にして学べば則ち老いて衰えず
老いて学べば則ち死して朽ちず

Those who study in their youth
will achieve something during their middle age years
Those who study in their middle age
will not decline in their old age
Those who study in their old age
will not be forgotten after their passing

We must learn the basics and foundation of life while we are still young. As we get older, we become busier with family and work obligations, and we tend to stop learning. We then start to lose our youthfulness which is called "Jakkyu (young but spiritless)." In contrast, older people who keep learning stay young and become more attractive.

The Aikido founder Morihei Ueshiba Sensei often said in his later years that his training had just begun. Shinryu Umeda Zenshi, the former head of Soto Sect, also used to say that he was an itinerant priest until the end of his life and enjoyed a green old age.

成功の秘訣を問うな
成すべき一つ一つに
全力を尽くせ

Do not ask me about the secret for success
Try your best to accomplish each and
every thing you must do

Josui Kuroda asked Hideyoshi,
"How did you get to where you are today?"

Hideyoshi replied,
"I never thought about promotion. All I did was to focus on my work and try to make it better every time."

Calligraphy by Tsuyoshi Inukai displayed in my dojo says as follows.
"Having a determination is the most important thing for everyone. If you are determined and focused, and try your best in every minute of your waking hours, you will eventually achieve your goal. Dedication is the key to success."

道は邇きに在り
而てこれを遠きに求む
事は易きに在り
而てこれを難きに求む

孟子

124

"The path of duty is near, and men seek it afar. The work of duty is easy, and men seek it in something difficult."

Mencius

When we visit a Zen temple, we often see a sign 脚下照顧 (kyakka-shoko) which literally means to light up at your feet. It is easy to see others, but we cannot understand at all when it comes to ourselves.

At his deathbed, the Buddha said,
"Let yourself be a light and rely upon yourself."
Dogen Zenji said something similar. "To learn the Buddhist Way is to learn about ourselves."

We tend to overlook the closest "self", and look for something far away.
We should be careful not to shut our eyes to our own shortcomings instead of looking elsewhere.
That reminds me of Morihei Ueshiba Sensei. He used to say that Aikido was a martial art of self improvement, not one to correct others."

あたり前のことを

あたり前に

Do the ordinary things in the ordinary way.

An Aikido master, Osawa Sensei, once sent me a New Year card with the message as saying to devote yourself to doing the ordinary things. It is easy to say, but hard to put into action.

A master of tea ceremony once asked Sen no Rikyu.
"What is the inner most secret of the tea ceremony?"
"Keep the atmosphere cool in summer and warm in winter. Lay the charcoal so it boils the water. Serve the tea to your guest's liking. That's all there is to it," he replied.

Doing the ordinary things in the ordinary way is easier said than done.

損は悟り
得は迷い

沢木興道

"Loss is enlightenment.
Gain is dellusion."

Kodo Sawaki

This teaching comes from Kodo Sawaki Roshi whom both Aikido master Kisaburo Osawa Sensei and Shinryu Umeda Zenji looked up to as their mentor.

Osawa Sensei and Umeda Zenji also told me the following over and over again.

"Nothing goes right for you when all you can think of is easy gain and you had done well. If you can remain calm even when you lose, you are quite a man."

"Now that I look back, that is a wise saying. If one can accept all his losses, he would be a great man. But in reality, nobody wants to lose. Instead, they are out looking for something good to gain. Become a man who can ignore his losses. It will be much easier on you."

From my book, "Jinsei Temaemochi (Life, on My Own Account)"

忙しい人の身心摂養法

喜神・感謝・陰徳

"Tips for good mental and physical health for busy people. Happiness, appreciation, and a secret act of charity."

This is what Masahiro Yasuoka Sensei suggested as a way for busy people to maintain and improve mental and physical health.

1. Always carry a Spirit of Happiness in your mind. No matter how hard things get, you should have some small space for the Happiness, deep in your heart. For example, should someone say something bad to you, attempt to slander or pass rumors behind your back, naturally you would get mad. However, deep inside your mind you should think, "Wait, this is actually a good opportunity for me to reflect upon myself. It will help me grow as a human being. Good, good."

2. Always be appreciative. Be thankful for everything that comes your way.

3. Always try to act charitably in secret. Aspire to do a good deed all the time, even when no one is looking. It does not matter how big or small it is, volunteer at every opportunity.

Happiness, appreciation, and a secret act of charity
It would be great if we could practice these in our life daily.

男は四十すぎたら
自分の顔に
責任をもたなければ
ならない

リンカーン

"Every man over forty is responsible for his face"

Abraham Lincoln

When a man asked Shoju Rojin (Hakuin Zenji's mentor) to give a ceremony to consecrate his Buddhist statue by inserting the eyes, Shoju Rojin said, "Instead of making a Buddhist statue, do something about your face."

It is often said that a great man in the old days cleansed his mind with words, and he carved his own face with the mental chisel. Those words are from the Analects of Confucius, Mencius, the Genshiroku, and they are the classic literature on the rules and principles of life.

Naoki Kojima

男子の顔色は
酒々落々の風懐が
なければならぬ

大久保利道

134

"A man should have free and easy manners."

Toshimichi Okubo

Before giving lectures, Eiji Yoshikawa, a writer, used to stop one station
before his destination and go to a restroom to massage his face.
When asked why he did it and he would answer,
"I wanted refresh myself before meeting someone for the first time."

「運命は性格の中にある」と言う言葉は等閑に生まれたものではない

芥川龍之介

"One's destiny lies within his personality. – a phrase like this is not a random remark."

Ryunosuke Akutagawa

Our destiny is necessity rather than coincidence. Ryunosuke Akutagawa said that the phrase, "One's destiny lies within his personality", is not a random remark. Woodrow Wilson, the 28th President of the United States, also said, "Our destiny does not happen by chance. People make their own destiny before facing it."

Every man is the architect of his own fortune.

Sallustius

溝はズンと跳べ
危ないと思うとはまるぞ

沢庵

138

"Jump over a ditch without hesitation. If you think it is dangerous, you will fall into it."

Takuan

Kaishu Katsu, one of the heroes in the late Tokugawa shogunate said.

"Whatever you do, go fearlessly. Do not hesitate, wondering whether you should do this or that. Do not think if it is easy or difficult. Be in the "state of selflessness" and take a decisive action. If you cannot succeed the first time, then keep trying until you succeed. People tend to lose patience too quickly and get tired before reaching their goal. That is why they cannot achieve a great success."

さしあたる
今日のことのみ思へただ
返らぬ昔知らぬゆく末

For the time being
Just think about today
As the past is gone, and the future is unknown

Shoju Rojin, Hakuin Zenji's mentor, once said.
"The most important thing is being mindful today, right now. If we neglect that, there is no tomorrow."

Everyone should know that today is an accumulation of each moment, and our lives are also an accumulation of every single day.

世の中に
人を育つる心こそ
我を育つる心なりけり

荒木田守武

142

A mind to nurture people for the society is also a mind to nurture oneself.

Moritake Arakida

You realize how much you can learn from teaching only when you are in a position to teach.
"To teach is to learn," isn't it?

I might make a mistake in my teaching.
I am worried about my students who trust me.

人の弱みを
ついてはいけません

山岡鉄舟

144

"Do not take advantage of someone's weakness."

Tesshu Yamaoka

Tesshu Yamaoka was a master of the swordsmanship, Zen and calligraphy. It seems that he was dauntless but kind at heart, and had a manly charm, which keep people attracted to him.

One of his apprentice, Tetsuju Ogura Sensei (The founder of Ichikukai dojo) also said, "It's mean to pick on another's weakness. To be a great man, a person must be considerate of the weakness in others and have a strong will not to give in to a strong man."(From Kamakura Yobanashi)

Everyone has something they do not want to talk about. It is perhaps the most important thing to remember in keeping company with others to perceive the most sensitive portion of another's feeling and to never mention it.

苟に日に新たにして
日々に新たに
又日に新たなり

If you can one day recreate yourself,
Do so from day to day.
Let there be daily recreation.

These are the words King Tang of Shang (Ancient China) carved onto the washtub he used every morning to wash his face in order to start his day afresh and improve himself every day. It means that we can cleanse our mind just like we wash ourselves in a washtub, to be better today than yesterday and tomorrow than today.

Hibari Misora's motto was "Tomorrow, I will be better than today." Morihei Ueshiba Sensei, the founder of Aikido, also used to say "Agatsu (to overcome temptation and to control yourself) is important.

二代目は
うしろ姿をよくまねる

The second generation copy their parents.

I remember reading this poem in "Masterpiece Selection of Salarymen's Senryu", or somewhere. I had a wry smile on my face because I felt like I was reading about myself.

A child didn't study much, so his father told him the story of George Washington.

"There is an impressive story about George Washington, being a good honest boy to his father when he was about your age. Why don't you study like him?"

Then, the child replied to his father,
"George Washington was a president when he was about your age."

今までは
人のことかと思いしに
わしが死ぬとは
こりゃたまらん

曽呂利新左衛門

"Up until now, I thought death was for other people. But now that I am dying, I can't stand it."

Shinzaemon Sorori

No matter how old you are, there seems to be no right age to end your life being completely satisfied. A wealthy old man asked Ryokan Osho.

"Although I have lived a very comfortable life, there is one thing that is beyond my reach. I am 80 years old now, but I want to live to 100 years old. Please show me how I can realize that."

Ryokan then said, "That's easy. Think of it as you have already lived 100 years. As you have already lived 100 years, any day after that is another day you gain. If you live one more year, you have gained another year after one hundred."

It is up to you whether you agree or dismiss it as a silly idea.

足るを知るは福の神
二匹鯛釣る
えびすなければ

仙厓

152

"The God od Wealth" knows what is enough
*Ebisu never fishes for two snappers

Sengai

There is one of Santoka's haiku.
Wash rice in a pot
Only one pot is enough

Santoka used to clean rice in a bucket of water, kept that water to do the dishes, then use that same water to wipe the floor. When he finished cleaning, he went to the field to water vegetables, while calling the name of the vegetables like "Spinach, Green onions." Although purchasing and spending were considered good, it is no longer the time to use and throw away things.

We know those days are over, yet people still waste a lot. I wonder if we can make the best use of our possessions.

The wind brings enough fallen leaves to make a fire.

Ryokan

* *Ebisu - The God of Wealth*

人並なら人並
人並はずれにゃ
人並はずれん

**Average is just average.
Unless you stand out,
You are never extraordinary.**

These are the words displayed on the wall of the classroom of my daughter's high school.

Kokichi Mikimoto, best known as Shinju-o (King of Pearl) once said, "For a man to become extraordinary, he has to completely absorb himself into one thing. If a man is mentally sick, then he is not sane. However, when a man does things others do not, or becomes really enthusiastic about his work, the general public treat him like he has gone mad. This is what I do not understand about those people."

何事も真剣にやれ

Do everything in earnest.

The following is one of the guiding principles at Takaba Juku where Mitsuru Toyama Sensei attended as a boy:

It's OK to sleep when you are sleepy.
Do your best when you are awake.
It is no good if you cannot tell whether someone is asleep or not.

君看よや雙眼の色
語らざるは
愁無きに似たり

Look at the shadow in both of my eyes, my friend
Silence conceal the sorrow

"Look deep into his eyes. It seems that he has no worries, troubles, pain, or sadness, as he does not share his feelings or talk about himself. But I can sense something like sorrows of life deep in his eyes."

Our life is full of pain and sadness. Even if we want to avoid them, they are often unavoidable.

It would be nice if we can stay strong enough to overcome them and even maintain a pleasant look on our face all the time without getting discouraged by such difficulties.

立ち並ぶ
慈眼仰げば御仏は
みな苦しみに
耐えし御姿

Though the rows of Buddhas have the merciful looks They are also bearing all the pains

In my mid-thirties, I accompanied the 2nd Doshu Kisshomaru Ueshiba Sensei on his trip to Yamaguchi. While we were having tea in one of the rooms at a Japanese-style hotel, Doshu said,

"Although it seems like people have no troubles in their lives and they look very happy, many of them quite often have concerns and pains. However, by overcoming those difficulties one by one, we can become a mature person."

His words really hit hard since I had seen him going through various troubles and hardships.

To this day, I still recall what he told me whenever I face problems, and really appreciate him for his words.

天を恨み
人を咎めることはあらじ
我が過ち思い返せば

Never blame Heaven or people
Look back at your own faults

I believe this is a poem written by Emperor Meiji.
"Life, on My Own Account" that are the words Shinryu Umeda Zenji (Zen master) often mentioned.
"I ended up like this because of him."
"I failed because I followed what he told me."
Others are not to be blamed.
If we humbly reflect on our conducts, we would realize that we are who we are now as the result of our own thoughts and actions.

A fiery car, there is no carpenter to make one,
One will ride on what he makes by himself.

実るほど頭を垂れる稲穂かな

The more rice an ear has
The lower it hangs

I was in my late 20s when I came to Kyushu.
Osawa Sensei from the headquarters sometimes called me and said,
"How are you doing? I don't have anything in particular to say, but I just wanted to hear your voice."
Then he always added,
"You are not being haughty, are you?"
"Is there such a rumour?" I asked.
"It would be too late then," he said.
Out of his parental love, he was concerned if a youngster like me had become the king of the mountain and big headed in Kyushu.
I am really fortunate to have had a mentor like him.
Now that my mentors who used to give me a piece of advice occasionally have all passed away,
I miss those days.

残心美し

Zanshin is beautiful.

Zanshin is a state of mind and body, where you are still focussed after you throw or pin down your opponent and prepared to be ready even if your opponent fights back. In our day-to-day life, this would be about concluding or winding up something;

Putting things in order after your work,

tidying up your desk after studying,

Cleaning up before leaving the washroom,

Making sure the fire is out before leaving your home,

Locking your house, etc...

As the proverb goes

"A bird does not foul the nest that it is about to leave

(Leave the place the way you wish to find it)."

When you leave a hotel, do you leave your bathrobe and towels in a disorderly manner? Do you leave things behind?

I once read that Kyuzo Mifune Sensei, a Judo master, always kept "Zanshin" in his mind.

悪いことはするな

いいことはしろ

Do not do bad things.
Do good things.

When Hakurakuten (Bai Yuyi), known as a poetic genius, asked Choka
Osho (Dorin Zenji) about the essence of Zen, he said, "Don't do bad things.
Do good things."
So he replied back,
"Even children would know that."
Choka Osho then admonished him,
"Although a three-year-old knows that, it is difficult even for an eighty year
old man to do that."
What you know and what you can do are different.

親あってこそ
師あってこそ友あってこそ
自分がある
ゆめゆめ自力とは思うまい

原田観峰

170

"Thanks to my parents, teachers, and friends,
I am who I am today.
Never think you did everything by yourself."

Kampo Harada

It is said that we realize what we owe to our parents only after becoming a parent ourselves. Only when we have our own children, we do realize how much love and affection we received from our parents, how hard it was for them to raise us, and that parents are a blessing.

I received countless lessons from so many teachers as well. I also have many friends that I shared joy, pain, and friendly rivalry with. I wonder what I can do to show my gratitude to those people who helped me grow up.

"When one wishes to be a good son, his parents are gone."

(Heaven would punish you if you say things like, "Though I have no interest in being a good child, my parents are still alive.")

One chance in a lifetime

"Ichigo-ichie (one time, one meeting)" refers to one chance in a lifetime.
In life, every moment is "Ichigo-ichie" as we can never have the same
"encounter" at the same "moment" again.
The encounter with "now" only happens once in our lifetime. Let's lead a
wonderful life valuing and appreciating that "now."

Live every day as though it were the last
Meeting only once in a while
Treasure every meeting, for it will never reoccur

Profile of Morito Suganuma

Born in Fukushima, Japan, his first contact with Aikido was in 1963 at Asia University in Tokyo where he trained under Nobuyoshi Tamura. He officially became an uchideshi under Morihei Ueshiba in 1967 after graduating from university.

A year after the death of Morihei Ueshiba, Suganuma was sent to Fukuoka by Kisshomaru Ueshiba as the Aikikai's representative for the Kyusyu district. He is the founder and dojocho of Aikido Shoheijuku Dojo, which today encompasses about 120 dojos. Although primarily based in Fukuoka, he is regularly invited to give Aikido seminars around the world. Seminar locations have included Vancouver, Norway, the Netherlands, Israel, and Beijing.

He received his 8th dan in 2001. He opened Tenjin Dojo of Shoheijuku in 2004. He is currently a committee member of All-Japan Aikido Federation.

He is also a well-known *Shodo master and regulary practices Zen mediation and Yoga.

*Shodo - Japanese Calligraphy

32428629R00107

Made in the USA
Charleston, SC
18 August 2014